Encountering the
Master Carpenter

Julia,

May the Master Carpenter
continue to build your
faith.

Brad Sinn

What others are saying about
Encountering the Master Carpenter

"These devotions by Brad Simon bring you into the scenes and experiences of the disciples as they listen to their Master teach them. The powerful messages can speak to the heart and shine light on Scripture that we may sometimes miss when we read the Bible. Each devotion is short enough to read through in a few minutes but will leave you with thoughts to contemplate throughout the day. I highly recommend this book."
- Barbara Latta, Christian Author

"Brad has a unique and insightful perspective that comes through with a clarity usual not seen in these types of stories. His writings have set me on a new course in my Christian endeavors to learn about Jesus and His disciples. His ability to tell a story brings new light to the characters that are highlighted. I find his writings draw me in and hold my attention from beginning to the end. Read and enjoy."
- Stephen H Dallas

"Part Max Lucado, part Josh McDowell, the devotions inspire you to build up faith by having intimate moments with Jesus."
- TA-MT, Amazon review

"The messages in this book are powerful because they are the truth of God. God has used this author to present stories from the four gospels in a colorful, easy to understand way that will be a blessing to anyone who will read and apply these truths to their lives. I've studied the Bible and taught Sunday school for decades, but after reading this book, I feel like I've gained a deeper understanding of various details that leads to a greater grasp of the important truths to be found there."
- Sandra Julian Barker

"Master Carpenter masterfully applies God's Word to the heart. Like a skilled craftsmen Simon takes Scripture and uses it like a tool to gently reshape the readers faith."
- Nick Ward

"Blending storytelling and biblical commentary, Brad Simon shares key lessons that Jesus imparted to his followers. Choosing passages from each of gospels, he imagines the scene and expounds on the lessons we can continue to apply in our lives today. Well written and organized. Excellent resource for those seeking uplifting messages or for those entering the faith Powerful stories in an extremely approachable setting."
- Sarah TX, Amazon review

"This book really brings the Bible to life in a more vivid way that helps you relate even better to all the characters.
- Ananta Ripa Ajmera"

"Brad's gift for storytelling is undeniable, breathing renewed life into the characters that grace the pages of his work. His narrative prowess captures my attention effortlessly, transporting me into the world he intricately weaves. From the very beginning to the final word, I am engrossed in his writings, a testament to his ability to engage and captivate his readers.

Engaging with Brad's writings has not only been a pleasure but a transformative experience. His unique approach has redefined my journey in understanding Jesus and His disciples. Every story he tells is a beacon of illumination, shedding light on the nuances of these historical figures. Without a doubt, Brad's work is an invitation to delve deeper, savoring each page and cherishing the profound insights he brings to life.
- Lucas Tran

"This book is easy to read, enjoyable, and informative. I recommend this book to anyone who wishes to strengthen their faith, and have a closer walk with our Lord and Savior."
- Marion Ritzema

Encountering the Master Carpenter

Devotional Portraits of Christ Building the Faith of His Disciples

Brad Simon

Published by:

Christian
Growth
Ministry

Encountering the Master Carpenter

Dedication

This book is dedicated to Debbie Simon, my best friend, my sweetheart, and my wife. She has provided me with loving support throughout my adult life and has been a valuable asset in my teaching ministry.

A Special Thanks to Beebe and Katy Kauffman at Lighthouse Bible Studies. Their encouragement, coaching, and training have helped me refine my style of writing and made me a better writer.

Table of Contents

Introduction

Grab a cup of coffee or favorite beverage and close the door to your room. Sit down, relax, and let your imagination take you back in time, on an exciting journey through the Gospels. In these short easy-to-read narratives, you will witness the transformation of twelve common, ordinary men as Jesus builds them into the confident, courageous church leaders that turned the world upside down.

As you read these devotions, I encourage you to prayerfully consider specific actions God is leading you to take. Our ultimate goal is to be application. Following each devotion, space is provided called Action Steps, for you to personalize the message. May your responses become a record filled with many discoveries and commitments along your magnificent journey in the Christian life.

It is my sincere desire and fervent prayer that through these narratives, you will experience the emotions and passions of the people involved in these Biblical accounts. But most of all, through them, you will gain a greater understanding of God's Word, grow in your faith, and walk closer with your Lord and Savior Jesus Christ.

Discover how the Carpenter from Nazareth still builds the Faith of those who follow Him. I present *Encountering the Master Carpenter*.

Brad Simon

Christians, Wise and Otherwise

Matthew 7:24-27

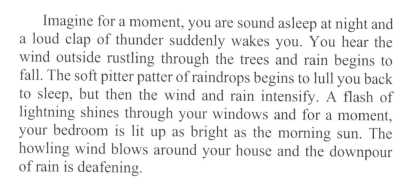

Imagine for a moment, you are sound asleep at night and a loud clap of thunder suddenly wakes you. You hear the wind outside rustling through the trees and rain begins to fall. The soft pitter patter of raindrops begins to lull you back to sleep, but then the wind and rain intensify. A flash of lightning shines through your windows and for a moment, your bedroom is lit up as bright as the morning sun. The howling wind blows around your house and the downpour of rain is deafening.

Then you feel it. Could it be? No, of course not. You were only dreaming, you reason. Go back to sleep, you tell yourself. But there it is again. Your house is moving!

You hear the cracking of plaster echoing through the house. Then there is a loud explosion of splintering lumber and bursting pipes. And your house comes crashing down around you! Far too late, you realize you built your house on a foundation of sand.

This is the illustration that Jesus used to close His longest recorded sermon. Matthew tells us that Jesus went up a mountain to get away from the multitudes. His followers came to Him, and He taught them (Matthew 5:1-2). Three chapters later, He finishes His teaching with these words.

> *"Therefore, everyone who hears these words of mine and acts on them will be like a wise man who built his house on the rock. The rain fell, the rivers rose, and the winds blew and pounded that house. Yet it didn't collapse, because its foundation was on the rock. But everyone who hears these words of mine and doesn't act on them will be like a foolish man who built his house on the sand. The rain fell, the rivers rose, the winds blew and pounded that house, and it collapsed. It collapsed with a great crash"* (Matthew 7:24-27).

Both builders in the parable are followers of Christ, both are Christians. The difference for them is not concerning salvation, but obedience after salvation. Jesus isn't speaking literally, but figuratively. The house they built is a reference to building a life, establishing values, and making decisions. It concerns our philosophy of life. Do we have a Biblical view of life built on the solid rock of God's Word, or a worldly view built on the shifting sands of human philosophy and opinions?

Both builders faced a storm of rain, floods, and winds. Again, the storm is not to be taken literally, but symbolically. It represents the storms of life. Jesus is telling us how to build our lives so that we can withstand the trials and calamities of life in this world.

Both builders listen to and heard the words of Jesus. The only difference is one little word. Jesus said, *everyone who hears these words of mine and acts on them will be like a wise man* (Matthew 7:24). Then He said, *everyone who hears these words of mine and doesn't act on them will be like a foolish man* (Matthew 7:26). The only difference is the wise man acts on what he hears, and the foolish man doesn't.

We can listen to storm warnings on the radio and TV all day long. But unless we get up out of our chair and do something, we will not be prepared, and tragedy may strike.

The same is true of the Christian life. We can listen to all the sermons in the world and read and study the Bible every day, but unless we apply the teachings to our lives and do what God instructs us to do, we become the Foolish Christians Jesus spoke about. If we do not trust Jesus enough to apply Biblical truth to our lives, then we will not be prepared to handle the storms of life. However, a builder who is wise hears the Word of God, applies it to his life, and as a result, stands firmly through turbulent times.

> When Moses instructed the nation Israel preparing them to enter the promised land, he said, *Look, today I set before you a blessing and a curse: there will be a blessing, if you obey the commands of the Lord your God I am giving you today, and a curse, if you do not obey the commands of the Lord your God.* (Deuteronomy 11:26-28)

Throughout the Old Testament, we read times when Israel obeyed God's Word and followed Him. God kept His promise and blessed the nation, and they were successful. Unfortunately, more often, the nation turned away from God and was not obedient to His Word and one calamity after another occurred. Eventually they were led away into captivity.

In the first century, as the church was spreading, James, a leader in the early church and half-brother to Jesus, wrote these words.

> *But be doers of the word and not hearers only, deceiving yourselves. Because if anyone is a hearer of the word and not a doer, he is like someone looking at his own face in a mirror. For he looks at himself, goes away, and immediately forgets what kind of person he was. But the one who looks intently into the perfect law of freedom*

and perseveres in it, and is not a forgetful hearer but a doer who works—this person will be blessed in what he does. (James 1:22-25)

All throughout the history of the Bible, God instructs His followers to apply His instructions to their lives, and He has promised many wonderful benefits to our lives if we are obedient in doing so. As 19th century evangelist and pastor R. A. Torrey said, "Blessings lie in the direction of obedience to God's commands. They are but signboards that mark the road to present success and blessedness and to eternal glory." [i]

Psalm 119 begins with these words:
How happy are those whose way is blameless, who walk according to the Lord's instruction! Happy are those who keep his decrees and seek him with all their heart. They do nothing wrong; they walk in his ways. You have commanded that your precepts be diligently kept. If only my ways were committed to keeping your statutes! Then I would not be ashamed when I think about all your commands. I will praise you with an upright heart when I learn your righteous judgments. I will keep your statutes; never abandon me. (Psalms 119:1-8)

Our spiritual foundation is vital to life. Spending time with God and submitting to His wisdom enables us to build a solid foundation based on His values. Then, when difficulties and uncertainties in life happen, when the floods of life overwhelm us, we can stand firm on the solid rock of God's Word and experience peace, joy, and stability.

Prayer:
Dear Heavenly Father, we come before Your throne in the authority of Your Son Jesus Christ our Lord and Savior. So often we read Your Word and close the cover, forgetting to apply it to our lives in obedience to You. Then, when

difficulties and uncertainties in life happen, as they so often do, we feel so overwhelmed.

Forgive us for being the unwise Christians Jesus spoke about, thinking we know better. May Your Holy Spirit fill us, inspire us, and strengthen us to walk worthy according to Your instruction. Our desire is to follow You and stand firmly on the solid rock of Your Word. We Praise You for the peace, joy, and stability in our lives that only You can bring. In Jesus name, we pray. Amen.

[i] R. A. Torrey, How to Succeed in the Christian Life, Revell, 1975, p. 60

Action Steps

How have you encountered the Master Carpenter through today's narrative?

_____

_____

_____

_____

What can you do to help others know this about Jesus?

_____

_____

_____

_____

_____

What might God be leading you to do based on this story in Scripture?

_____

_____

_____

_____

_____

Expanding Our Perspectives

John 4:1-42

The road was rough and rugged, and the air was dry and dusty. As the scorching sun reached its apex in the noontime sky, drops of sweat rolled down their faces, dripping from their beards. Jesus and His disciples had already hiked over twenty miles, crossing mountainous terrain in an unfamiliar land. Tired and hungry, the disciples went to buy food as Jesus sat down to rest.

They left Judea on their way to Galilee. This is a trip they had made before, but this time was different. This time, Jesus was determined to travel through Samaria. It was a land the Jews avoided, because of the great hatred between the Jews and Samaritans. It was greater than the feud between the Hatfields and the McCoys of America folklore, or the Montagues and the Capulets from Shakespeare's Romeo and Juliet.

The feud started 700 years before Christ. During the Assyrian captivity, many of the Israelites intermarried with their pagan captors and adopted much of their idolatrous worship practices. As they returned from captivity, they settled in Samaria. The Jews never forgave their brethren for this grievous sin and considered these half-breeds as heathen (2 Kings 17).

The hatred intensified during Nehemiah's rebuilding of Jerusalem's wall. Sanballat, the governor of Samaria, and his army opposed the rebuilding of the wall. They taunted and fought against the Jews, doing everything they could to stop the work (Nehemiah 4:1-8).

Jews traveled the longer routes to the east or west just to avoid the Samaritans. Their hatred was so intense that if the shadow of a Samaritan touched a Jew, they would need ceremonial cleansing at the temple.

But Jesus had a purpose for this trip, a lesson the disciples needed to learn. At His ascension, He told the disciples *you will be my witnesses in Jerusalem, in all Judea and Samaria, and to the ends of the earth* (Acts 1:8). If the Gospel was ever to spread beyond the Jewish nation, these men needed to overcome their deep-seated racial prejudice. A lesson that would indeed take a long time to learn.

Leaving early in the morning, Jesus and His disciples journeyed a great distance in the cool of the day. By noon, they reached Sychar, where Jacob had dug a well. They were hungry and weary from their journey, and Jesus sat by the well to rest while the disciples went to buy food. Imagine what a humbling experience this was for them. These Jewish men were probably more focused on dancing between the shadows and yet they had to buy food prepared and sold by the hated Samaritans.

While the disciples were off learning their first lesson of the day, an unusual visitor approached Jesus. In those days, women drew water from the well in the evening. But this woman came to draw water in the heat of the day, to avoid the other women in town. One or more adulterous relationships ended each of her five marriages and was now living with yet another man to whom she was not married. She probably did not get along with the women very well, because she got along too well with the men.

Jesus, thirsty from His journey, asked the woman for a drink. As the conversation developed between them, it is interesting to see the progression of her understanding of Jesus by the names she used for Him:

> *You Jew* (v. 9)
> *Sir* (v. 11&15)
> *A Prophet* (v. 19)
> *Messiah, the Christ* (v. 25)

When the disciples returned, it amazed them He was talking with a woman. Seeing the disciples, she left her water jar and went into town. Jesus told His Disciples, *"Look, I tell you, lift up your eyes, and see that the fields are white for harvest. ... I sent you to reap that for which you did not labor. Others have labored, and you have entered into their labor"* (John 4:35, 38 ESV).

When the woman at the well told the people in Sychar about Jesus, they came to see Him. As the disciples lifted their eyes, the road and fields were covered in white from all the Samaritans coming over the hillside dressed in their long white robes. They also were ripe for a spiritual harvest, as they were ready to believe. They just needed someone to teach them.

For the next two days, they stayed in this community, and the story closes with these words. *Many more believed because of what he said. And they told the woman, "We no longer believe because of what you said, since we have heard for ourselves and know that this really is the Savior of the world"* (John 4:41-42).

Nowhere in the New Testament do we find such a city-wide revival. Not since Jonah preached to Nineveh did an entire city repent of their sinful ways and turn to the living God. But do you notice something missing from this narrative?

13

Jesus instructed His followers to disciple the people of Sychar (John 4:35-38). Yet there is no mention of them during their two-day stay. Instead, we read of this nameless, immoral Samaritan woman, being obedient to Jesus, sharing her newfound faith. Truly, this was a time when the woman at the well, out discipled the disciples!

The disciples were slow in their understanding and failed their lesson on this day. Years later, it took a vision from the Lord and the working of the Holy Spirit for Peter to finally overcome his prejudices (Acts 10). But when they fully comprehended the Lord's teachings, there were no shadows they avoided, no person they did not reach and touch with the love of God.

Under the inspiration of the Holy Spirit, the Apostle Paul wrote, *there is no Jew or Greek, slave or free, male and female; since you are all one in Christ Jesus* (Galatians 3:28). There is to be no racial, sexual, economic, social, political, or any other division in Christ. Instead of looking down at those different from us, we are to see as God sees and look inward at their heart. *Humans do not see what the Lord sees, for humans see what is visible, but the Lord sees the heart* (1 Samuel 16:7).

My brothers and sisters, do not show favoritism as you hold on to the faith in our glorious Lord Jesus Christ (James 2:1). Far too often, we live our Christian lives as the disciples did during these two days. Instead, we need to change our perspective of people and follow the example of the Samaritan woman at the well.

Prayer:
Dear Heavenly Father, forgive us for all the times we judge people because they differ from us. Help us to not look at outward appearance, but to see people as Your children. Help us love one another just as You love us.

As Jesus saw the multitudes as sheep without a shepherd and with compassion in His heart ministered to them, may we reach out in compassionate love to touch the lives of those around us regardless of their social status or nationality. In Christ's name, we pray. Amen.

Action Steps

Date _____

How have you encountered the Master Carpenter through today's narrative?

_____

_____

_____

_____

What can you do to help others know this about Jesus?

_____

_____

_____

_____

What might God be leading you to do based on this story in Scripture?

_____

_____

_____

_____

_____

Peace Beyond Understanding

Matthew 8:23-27, Mark 4:35-41, Luke 8:22-25

It was a calm, peaceful night, and the moon cast a silvery streak across the black water. The stillness of the air was matched by the quiet water below. The boats sailed smoothly across the Sea of Galilee as if sliding on a sheet of glass. There was not a cloud in the dark sky and the men could easily navigate their boats by the stars that filled the heavens. They felt right at home as most of them were professional fishermen and had sailed these waters many times at night while fishing. Jesus was in the boat along with His twelve disciples. They were midway across the sea without a care in the world. But then it happened.

The wind rushed down the side of the mountain and across the sea, and a fierce storm erupted. The hurricane-like winds caused the waves to sweep over the boat, drenching the men inside. This was no ordinary storm like these men faced many times on their fishing expeditions. Terror gripped the men. They feared a watery grave with their boat as their casket awaited them. As the men struggled for their lives, Jesus slept soundly in the corner with the waves rocking the boat like a cradle.

The day had started like many others. Jesus was teaching His disciples along the shore of the sea when a large crowd gathered. The multitude was so great that Jesus asked His disciples to get a boat for Him to sit in, so all could hear as He taught the people. Later, as the crowd dispersed, Jesus spent time with His disciples explaining the meaning of the parables. Now it was time for a test to see if they learned the lesson Jesus taught them. When evening came, He said, *"Let's cross over to the other side of the sea"* (Mark 4:35).

The omniscient Lord knew the storm was coming and certainly could have prevented it. But He permitted the storm to happen and sent His disciples out on the water, providing the perfect opportunity for a pop quiz.

Many Christians believe that difficulties in life come when we disobey God. But that is not always the case. Sometimes God uses a crisis to discipline His children. Jonah ended up in a storm at sea because of his disobedience. But here the disciples found themselves in a storm because they obediently followed the Lord's instruction.

Like the disciples on that day, today we hear the Word of God taught in large gatherings in our church services and small group Bible studies. We spend time alone with God in prayer and through our personal reading and studying of Scripture. This all leads to our spiritual growth, but true Christian maturity rarely occurs until our faith is tested. James tells us, *the testing of your faith produces endurance. And let endurance have its full effect, so that you may be mature and complete, lacking nothing* (James 1:3-4). It is not enough to learn Biblical truth. We must be able to put those lessons into practice. Our faith needs to be tested to produce Christian maturity in our lives.

When the terrifying storm convinced the disciples they were about to die, they forgot one important factor; Jesus was in the boat, and He told them they were going to the other side of the sea. They experienced needless fear because

20

they did not trust the words of Jesus. He did not promise a peaceful trip, but He assured them of their destination.

While the disciples feared for their lives, Jesus could sleep because He rested confidently in the will of His Father. When they finally awakened Jesus, He spoke to the wind, and the wind obeyed the voice of its maker. Jesus *got up, rebuked the wind, and said to the sea, "Silence! Be still!" The wind ceased, and there was a great calm* (Mark 4:39).

The lesson Jesus wanted the disciples to learn from this test was that God is bigger than any problems they would face, and they only needed to put their trust in Him. Jesus calling them *you of little faith* (Matthew 8:26) does not imply that they need more faith. Later, Jesus will tell them *if you have faith the size of a mustard seed* (Matthew 17:20). It is not a matter of how much faith you have, but who you have your faith in. Jesus' statement revealed that the disciples still had faith in what they believed to be a little God. Their understanding was of a God too small to overcome the obstacle they faced.

The Apostle Paul tells us, *set your minds on things above, not on earthly things* (Colossians 3:2). The world tells us to worry and fear. Every newscast gives us something else to worry about. Politicians constantly remind us to fear the opposition party. Gloom and doom are spread over social media like wildfire. However, God tells us *Don't worry* (Matthew 6:25), *Be anxious for nothing* (Philippians 4:6), and *Fear not* (Isaiah 41:10).

The disciples failed their test. Their problem was not the storm surrounding them, but the doubt within them. The disciples dwelt on earthly things. They looked around them and saw the danger of the storm. They looked within and saw fear. But they failed to look up by faith and see God.

The Prophet Isaiah called Jesus the *Prince of Peace* (Isaiah 9:6). Jesus told us, *Peace I leave with you. My peace I give to you* (John 14:27). In place of fear and worry, we can experience *the peace of God, which surpasses all understanding* (Philippians 4:7). Not always an absence of conflict but a peaceful, calm assurance—a tranquil spirit amid the crisis. An acknowledgement that God is in control. It's been said, "Sometimes God calms the storm, sometimes He lets the storm rage and calms His child." [i]

When the Apostle Paul was caught in a storm at sea, rather than calm the storm as He did on the Sea of Galilee, the storm continued for fourteen days. While the sea raged and battered the ship, and hope of being saved was fading, Paul exhibited a calm, peaceful, tranquil spirit (Acts 27:13-37).

No matter what life's difficulties we go through, we can confidently prevail, resting on the promise that God is with us. *Even when I go through the darkest valley, I fear no danger, for you are with me* (Psalm 23:4).

Peter certainly learned his lesson. After the Apostle James was martyred, Peter sat in prison in anticipation of his execution. But rather than fret and worry about his life as he did in the boat on the Sea of Galilee, he rested peacefully, knowing his life was in the hands of God, not King Herod. He slept so soundly the angel had to strike him to wake him and instruct him to get dressed. Outside the prison, he was still half asleep as he followed the angel and thought it was all a dream (Acts 12:1-10).

When the storms of life come crashing down around us, as they often will, we need to look past our circumstances and ignore the world's cries for worry and concern. Instead, we are to look heavenward and listen to the Lord's command to *fear not* and rest confidently in the peace of God promised to us. Knowing that God's omnipotent power is greater than any of this world's problems.

Prayer:

Dear Father, forgive us for all the time we needlessly fret and worry. For all the times the storms of life cause us to doubt, and we dwell on earthly things, listening to everything the world tells us to fear. While our life on this earth is not free from difficulties, You promised us to use those trials for our good, to bring us to maturity in our walk with You.

When the storms of life come crashing down around us and our circumstances seem to spiral out of control, help us bring our cares and concerns to You and trust in Your Word. Help us rely on You to guide us through the storm and follow Jesus' example resting in Your arms, entrusting ourselves to Your tender care and mercies. May Your peace and comfort surround us as we live confidently knowing You are in control of all our circumstances. Provide in us a tranquil spirit, knowing that You do indeed love and care for us. In Christ's name, we pray, Amen.

[i] Original source unknown, attributed to a variety of different authors on the Internet.

Action Steps

How have you encountered the Master Carpenter through today's narrative?

_____

_____

_____

_____

_____

What can you do to help others know this about Jesus?

_____

_____

_____

_____

_____

What might God be leading you to do based on this story in Scripture?

_____

_____

_____

_____

_____

Hanging on by a Thread

Matt 9:18-26, Mark 5:21-43, Luke 8:40-56

Dishonored, discouraged, depressed, but most of all, she was desperate. The people dejected and despised her. For twelve long, agonizing years, she suffered from a continual, unrelenting flow of blood. She was physically exhausted and socially excluded. She had spent all her money on physicians who failed to help her. She was bankrupt financially, physically, socially, and emotionally.

It also affected her spiritually. According to the law of Moses, she was unclean and not allowed into the temple to worship her God. She was hanging on to life by a thread.

Then she heard that a miracle worker from Nazareth named Jesus and His disciples had arrived. "Maybe, just maybe, if I touch His garment," she thought, "I could be healed." A crowd of people had already gathered so closely compacted it would make most people claustrophobic. When she finally found Jesus, He already appeared to have His mind set on a task and seemed determined to accomplish it.

Earlier Jairus, a leader in the synagogue, had approached Jesus. Falling on his knees before Him, he pleaded with Jesus to come to his home and heal his dying daughter. Despite the crowd crushing in on them, Jesus and His disciples wound their way through the maze of people to reach Jairus' home.

The events that transpired are the only intertwined miracles recorded in the Gospels. Two people as different as different could be, linked together for all of history. The dramatic contrast between the two is striking:

> ➢ He was well known; she was a nameless face in the crowd.
> ➢ He was wealthy; she was poor.
> ➢ He was a leading citizen; she was an outcast.
> ➢ He was a religious leader; she was not allowed in the synagogue.
> ➢ He was interceding for his only child; she was seeking help for herself.
> ➢ He had experienced twelve years of joy and happiness; she had experienced twelve years of misery and sorrow.

Yet, as different as they were, both Jairus and the poor woman were hanging on to life by a thread. Both seeking the healing touch of Jesus' hand.

As the crowd pressed in around them, making it difficult to walk, Jesus spoke. *"Who touched me?"* (Luke 8:45). At first, His words appeared sarcastic, as if He was scolding the people for keeping Him from His work. But then they seemed more amusing than cynical. "The crowd is unrelenting. Everyone is bumping into us and touching us. What are You talking about?" The disciples must have thought.

"It was I", a voice said so soft and meek it could hardly be heard above the murmur of the crowd. The disciples turned and only saw the mass of people. As Jesus turned, His eyes fixed on the woman kneeling at His feet, trembling before Him.

In the presence of all the people, she declared the reason she had touched him and how she was instantly healed. "Daughter," he said to her, "your faith has saved you. Go in peace."

While he was still speaking, someone came from the synagogue leader's house and said, "Your daughter is dead. Don't bother the teacher anymore." When Jesus heard it, he answered him, "Don't be afraid. Only believe, and she will be saved. (Luke 8:47-50)

Despite Jesus' promise, the news of the death of his only child must have struck Jairus hard. Agony and anguish surely flooded his soul. Jairus' friends and colleagues were among the religious leaders that opposed Jesus. Going to Jesus for help will certainly cause him conflict. Saving his daughter was more important to him than losing some friends, but what good is that now?

When they reached the house of Jairus, they *saw the flute players and a crowd lamenting loudly* (Matthew 9:23). The family and friends had gathered, joined by professional mourners expressing their grief. The best they thought Jesus could do now would be to express some kind words about Jairus' daughter and comfort their sorrow. Jesus had words all right. Not **about** the girl, but **for** the girl.

"Little girl, I say to you, get up" (Mark 5:41). The next thing anyone knew, she was walking and eating, the family was rejoicing, and the hired mourners were sent home early.

These intertwined miracles reflect different aspects of growth in the various characteristics of our faith. The woman needed reassurance and confidence. Jesus calling her out in the crowd of people required her to testify to an embarrassing situation. When Jesus called for her to step forward, she came trembling and spoke. Sometimes it's frightening to speak up for the Lord. But this woman found the strength and courage to overcome her fears. Her faith allowed her to tell the story of what Jesus had done for her.

While the woman's faith needed strengthening because she was shy, Jairus' faith required patience in waiting for the Lord. It was easier for Jairus to trust the Lord while his daughter was still alive, and Jesus was walking with him. But the crowd hindered their progress, then this woman dared to interfere and stop Jesus for her healing. By the time his friend arrived with news of his daughter's death, no doubt Jairus felt the thread of hope he was hanging onto was unraveling.

Jairus was desperate, and he needed all the encouragement he could get. Jesus assured him saying, *"Don't be afraid. Only believe"* (Mark 5:36). And the resulting miracle was beyond anything he could have imagined.

Both had faith that Jesus could heal, but their faith needed to grow. She was asked to bring her faith out of its shell; he was challenged to have a faith that trusted and persisted. Her timid faith needed to rely on God's strength and boldness. His anxious faith needed to rely on God's peace and patience.

Often, our faith gives way to doubts when circumstances and feelings overwhelm us. Sometimes God delays, and we wonder why. Why did Jesus wait to go to Jairus' house to heal his daughter? Why didn't He heal her from a distance like He did the centurion's servant (Matthew 8:5-12), or the nobleman's son (John 4:46-54)? Why does God answer immediately some things that seem less urgent, and delays in answering what we feel is most crucial?

These two intertwined narratives powerfully illustrate how God provided each person exactly what they needed, when they needed it. And He will do the same for us if we go to Him, as they did, and seek His guidance.

Prayer:

Dear Father, so often it seems like we are hanging on to life by a thread. We see You answering prayers of others and wonder why You delay in answering ours. Thank You for seeing where our faith is weak and moving in our lives in ways that we don't understand. But through it all, You are working to build us up and transform our lives into the image of Your Son. In His name, we pray. Amen.

Action Steps

How have you encountered the Master Carpenter through today's narrative?

_____

_____

_____

_____

_____

What can you do to help others know this about Jesus?

_____

_____

_____

_____

_____

What might God be leading you to do based on this story in Scripture?

_____

_____

_____

_____

_____

The Most Prized Possession

Matthew 13:44-46

He stood in stunned silence. Instinctively, his hands rose to rub his eyes. Were they deceiving him? Could what he is seeing really be true?

With trembling hands, he carefully reached out and placed it on the back of his fingers. Slowly and gently, he tipped his hand, rolling it back and forth. From every angle, the sphere's symmetry was perfect. The creamy white color exhibited undertones of rose and there was not a single spot or blemish on the surface. The intense luster produced an iridescent glow that begged to be touched. Its alluring beauty was beyond compare. In all his years buying and selling pearls, he had never experienced seeing one as magnificent as this, and his heart longed to possess it.

Throughout His ministry, Jesus used such illustrations to teach His disciples about the Kingdom of God. Here the pearl merchant had searched all his life for that one special pearl of great value, and in the sister parable, a man stumbled upon a treasure buried in a field.

Some people, like the merchant, spend their lives searching for God before they discover the truth of Scripture. While others, like the man in the field, without seeking it, stumble upon the truth of God's Word and immediately recognize its value. In both parables, the result is the same. They sell all that they have so they can possess their discovery. By doing so, they are gaining something far more valuable than any of their possessions, something worth far more than any sacrifice one might make to acquire it.

The point Jesus is making is not on buying your way into the kingdom, but on recognizing its supreme value. He was not teaching that salvation could be bought, but rather the cost of true discipleship. Jesus' death on the cross paid the full price of our salvation and it is given as a free gift to us by the grace of God. However, if we are truly to follow Him, we must give all that we have and all that we are to Him.

There is nothing wrong with having earthly possessions and developing close personal relationships. God graciously provides good things for us to enjoy in this life. King Solomon said, *It is appropriate to eat, drink, and experience good in all the labor one does under the sun during the few days of his life God has given him, because that is his reward* (Ecclesiastes 5:18). And Paul said, *God richly provides us with all things to enjoy* (1Timothy 6:17). However, Jesus' disciples are to understand that there is nothing in this world more valuable than to possess the Kingdom of God.

Author Wilbur Rees wrote about the casual attitude many Christians exhibit. "I would like to buy $3 worth of God, please, not enough to explode my soul or disturb my sleep, but just enough to equal a cup of warm milk or a snooze in the sunshine. I want ecstasy, not transformation; I want the warmth of the womb, not a new birth. I want a pound of the Eternal in a paper sack. I would like to buy $3 worth of God, please." [i]

Jesus said *every one of you who does not renounce all his possessions cannot be my disciple* (Luke 14:33). Jesus doesn't beat around the bush. He gets straight to His point. To be His disciple requires us to make Jesus the first priority in our life, ahead of our possessions and relationships.

Later, Peter asked Jesus, *"Look, we have left what we had and followed you." So he said to them, "Truly I tell you, there is no one who has left a house, wife or brothers or sisters, parents or children because of the kingdom of God, who will not receive many times more at this time, and eternal life in the age to come."* (Luke 18:28-30)

God's plan for His resources differs with each one of us. Today, God calls some of His disciples to full-time missionary work. Like Peter and the Apostles, they leave their homes and family behind to serve God. For others, like Mary the mother of John Mark, God calls them to use their earthly possessions for the good of His Kingdom (Acts 12:11-19). Still others, like Barnabas, are called to use their resources to finance God's Kingdom (Acts 4:32-37). In whatever way God directs us, we can be assured that the eternal rewards we receive in Heaven, dwarf whatever temporary pleasure and enjoyment we might gain from our earthly possessions.

The apostle Paul said, *I have been crucified with Christ, and I no longer live, but Christ lives in me. The life I now live in the body, I live by faith in the Son of God, who loved me and gave himself for me.* (Galatians 2:20)

Jesus did not die on the cross for us, so we can go on living our lives as we choose. The Christian life is a life of continual dependence on Him, yielding our desires to Him and allowing Christ to live through us.

Jesus calls us into a relationship, not just a decision. God's grace brings salvation as a gift but included is a wonderful journey of walking with Him. God doesn't want Christians to be satisfied with $3 worth of Him. He doesn't want us to be content with being saved, that is only the beginning. He desires for us to enter a relationship with Him and begin a lifetime journey of discipleship, trusting Him, and following His will for our lives. No one can know what God desires from us at the start of the journey, but as we daily walk with Him, He reveals His plan one step at a time.

Our Heavenly Father owns everything. We are simply managers of what He has entrusted to us. We must always remember whose they are when He calls for us to surrender them for work in His Kingdom. Hymn writer Judson Van DeVenter said it so well, "All to Jesus I surrender, all to Him I freely give. I will ever love and trust Him, in His presence daily live. All to Jesus I surrender, humbly at His feet I bow. Worldly pleasures all forsaken, take me Jesus take me now. I surrender all. All to Thee my blessed Savior, I surrender all." [ii]

No sacrifice we can make is too great to live in God's will and experience a discipleship relationship with Him. The Apostle Paul certainly understood the surpassing value of this relationship. He said, *I also consider everything to be a loss in view of the surpassing value of knowing Christ Jesus my Lord* (Philippians 3:8).

Missionary Jim Elliot wisely said, "He is no fool who gives what he cannot keep to gain that which he cannot lose." [iii]

Prayer:
Most gracious Heavenly Father, we are thankful for all the riches and blessings You have given us. Forgive us for all the times we see them as ours and go through life oblivious to what we could accomplish for Your Kingdom. Help us put Your Work here on earth above our selfish desires and pleasures. Help us see the surpassing value Your Kingdom brings to us and to those around us. May we always strive to make Jesus our first priority, in His Name we pray. Amen.

[i] Wilbur Rees, "$3.00 Worth of God," as quoted by Charles R. Swindoll in Discipleship Ministry Up Close and Personal (Fullerton, CA, Insight for Living, 1990) p. 35

[ii] I Surrender All, Judson W. Van DeVenter, 1896, Public Domain

[iii] journal entry for October 28, 1949, Jim Elliot

Action Steps

Date _____

How have you encountered the Master Carpenter through today's narrative?

_____

_____

_____

_____

What can you do to help others know this about Jesus?

_____

_____

_____

_____

What might God be leading you to do based on this story in Scripture?

_____

_____

_____

_____

_____

A Step of Faith

Matt 14:22-33, Mark 6:45-52, John 6:16-21

The moonlight glistened across the still water, and a slight breeze added a freshness to the early evening air. It would be a short peaceful boat ride across the Sea of Galilee, a much-needed break for the disciples from several demanding weeks of ministering to the people.

Early that morning, Jesus and His disciples went to a desolate place beside the Sea of Galilee to be alone. It was to be a day to rest, however, a large crowd found them and followed. Five thousand men plus women and children, over twenty thousand people gathered around them.

Seeing the multitude, Jesus had compassion on them. Instead of a day of rest and relaxation, it was yet another long day of healing the sick and teaching the people. The day concluded with one of the most famous miracles. Jesus fed the multitude with five loaves of bread and two fish.

As the people departed, Jesus sent the disciples on ahead while He dismissed the crowd and went to the mountain to pray. Finally, they experienced the time away from the multitudes they desperately needed. But just as quickly as their day had changed from one of rest to a long day of work, their quiet, peaceful boat ride would turn most unexpectedly.

The cheerful moon that lit their course was soon hidden behind the clouds and the cool crisp breeze turned into the fierce wind of a turbulent storm. As the waves crashed against the side of the boat, the disciples, most of whom were professional fishermen, struggled to keep the boat on course.

After hours of strenuous rowing, long after they should have arrived at the other side, they had barely covered half the journey. It was now the middle of the night and darkness closed in around them while the unrelenting wind pounded the waves violently against the boat. Tired and exhausted, their muscles ached with every movement. Their fingers and arms grew numb from rowing. All alone without their Lord to comfort them, fear gripped the disciples.

Then, from nowhere, it appeared. "Did you see that?" someone whispered. "See what?" came the reply. "Over there on the waves. It looks like a person." He answered. "You're tired, you're just hallucinating."

"No. I see it too," said another. "It, it looks like a ghost." "You're both crazy!" replied another disciple. "Quit making excuses and get back to rowing." As the storm continued to rage, the disciples' fear intensified.

Jesus was walking on the water toward them, but they did not recognize Him because they focused on themselves and their difficult situation. They were in a storm and fearing for their lives, not looking for Jesus. Fear and faith cannot live in the same heart.

Jesus knew the storm would come. Yet He deliberately sent the disciples on ahead, out in a boat into the storm. Why? Because He had a lesson to teach them. The disciples needed to learn that even though Jesus wasn't physically present, He was watching and praying for them. Jesus waited until the boat was as far from land as possible so that all human hope was gone. Then He walked on the water to show His disciples the very thing they feared was only a footpath for Him to come to them.

While it may be difficult to understand at the time, we are actually safer in the storm in God's will. than on dry land outside of God's will. We should never judge our security based on our circumstances alone.

Immediately Jesus spoke to them. "Have courage! It is I. Don't be afraid." "Lord, if it's you," Peter answered him, "command me to come to you on the water." He said, "Come" (Matthew 14:27-29a).

Peter stepped out of the boat and walked on the water toward Jesus. As he steps out of the boat in the middle of the storm, I can just imagine Peter as he lifts his foot to step over the side of the boat thinking, "what in the world did I get myself into this time?" But he had enough faith to step out of the boat and he walked on the water. What an awesome experience that must have been!

As he was walking on the water, a wave came up in front of him and he could no longer see Jesus. He became frightened and began to sink. Peter cried out to Jesus, *"Lord, save me!" Immediately Jesus reached out his hand, caught hold of him, and said to him, "You of little faith, why did you doubt?"* (Matthew 14:30b-31).

They got into the boat and the disciples believed in Jesus. That is what Jesus wanted them to learn, to have faith in Him. Nothing is impossible for Him to accomplish. He could feed twenty-some thousand people with five crackers and two fish. He could walk on water. He could calm a storm. Nothing was impossible for Him.

I think it is interesting to note that when Peter realized it was Jesus walking on the water, he did not just jump up and step out of the boat. He first asked Jesus, *"Lord, if it is you, command me to come to you on the water."*, and Jesus said, *"Come"* (Matthew 14:28-29). I think that is important because we need to look to God first to get direction from Him.

Billy Graham once said, "Instead of asking God to bless our plans, ask Him instead to show you His plans, and then give you the strength to follow them." [i]

We should always ask Jesus what His plans are for us. Then, when God reveals His plans, we can ask to be a part of them. Then and only then can we step out in faith. We are to put our faith in Jesus and step out of the boat. You can't walk on water if you stay in the boat! You must take that step of faith.

Once we step out in faith, the storms of life will come. Satan doesn't want us walking with Jesus. In the dark of the night, we will hear the wind whistling. We'll hear the waves as they beat against the side of the boat. The waves will try to distract us from Jesus. But we need to keep our eyes on Jesus and not on the surrounding circumstances.

Sometimes it is the people left in the boat who try to discourage us. We are walking with Jesus and those that don't have the faith to step out themselves will question us. They ask us what we are doing? Telling us it is not normal. They plead with us to come back in the boat. They need us to do our part and row the boat. The people left in the boat will often try to get us to stop walking with Jesus.

We must keep our eyes on Jesus. It is when Peter took his eyes off Jesus that he started to sink into the water. Your faith is strongest when you focus on His power and His love. The disciples struggled to row across the lake, but Jesus walked on top of the waves. When we focus on the surrounding problems, we doubt God's power.

Nothing changed about Jesus. It was Peter's doubt that caused him to sink. James wrote, *but let him ask in faith without doubting. For the doubter is like the surging sea, driven and tossed by the wind. That person should not expect to receive anything from the Lord, being double-minded and unstable in all his ways* (James 1:6-8).

44

We need to:
- ➤ Put our faith in Jesus.
- ➤ Seek His guidance, His plan for our life. Peter was the only disciple to walk on the water with Jesus because he was the only one who asked.
- ➤ Then we need to step out in faith and follow Him. We need to always keep our eyes on Jesus and not get distracted by our circumstances, nor listen to those still in the boat.
- ➤ Then as we are walking with Him, we can encourage others to step out in faith with us.

It's one thing for us to say we believe in God. Genuine faith is when we believe in God and put our faith and trust in His Son, Jesus Christ.

Unfortunately, today there are many Christians who say they believe in God. Like the disciples, they have a head knowledge of Him, and they sit in their boats rowing hard because that is what they had always done. It's comfortable in the boat.

But when God asks them to put that belief into action, to step out of the boat, just like the disciples, their faith is lacking. Genuine belief is believing in your heart, not just your head. It's putting your hope and trust in God and relying on Him to step out in faith when He calls. It's when we put our faith into action and step out of the boat like Peter we can walk with Jesus above the waves of the storm.

Prayer:

Dear Father, forgive us for all the times we did not put our faith in You. When we did not trust You and instead cowered in fear from the storms of life. Instead of being discouraged and fearful because of the surrounding circumstances, give us the strength to step out in faith and walk with You above our circumstances. Rather than listening to those still in the boat, inspire us to be an encouragement to them to take that step of faith and trust You to walk with us. And together we can serve You and minister together, bring glory to Your name. In Jesus' name we pray, Amen.

[i] Billy Graham, article *Ask God to Show You His Plan*, billygraham.ca/answer/ask-god-to-show-you-his-plans-not-bless-your-dreams

Action Steps

Date _____

How have you encountered the Master Carpenter through today's narrative?

_____

_____

_____

_____

_____

What can you do to help others know this about Jesus?

_____

_____

_____

_____

_____

What might God be leading you to do based on this story in Scripture?

_____

_____

_____

_____

_____

The Bread of Life

Matthew 14:13-21, Mark 6:30-44, Luke 9:10-17, John 6: 1-15, 22-59

As the weeks turned into months, the popularity of Jesus grew. Wherever He and His disciples went, the crowds pressed in around them. Early one morning, they sailed across the Sea of Galilee to a desolate place to be alone. They desired a quiet time for a little rest and relaxation.

The disciples had just returned from being sent out to minister on their own for the first time. One can imagine, their feet were sore, and their bodies ached from walking from town to town over rocky roads through the mountains. But more than needing physical rest, they were mentally exhausted from the long days of ministering to the people.

The cool breeze as they sailed was so refreshing, and as they stepped out of their boat on the eastern shore, the fragrance of the wildflowers filled the air with a sweet aroma. The leaves on the olive trees fluttered in the breeze, as if waving to welcome the weary travelers.

But they were not alone for long. The crowd of people learned where they went and followed. Others came from nearby towns. Before long, there were 5,000 men besides women and children. Most likely, there were over 20,000 people in total gathered along the seashore.

When Jesus saw the crowd, He had compassion on them and saw them as sheep without a shepherd. Jesus began teaching them and healing everyone who had a need. He preached not only through the lunch hour, but He taught all the way through supper!

It was now getting late in the day and the disciple came to Jesus asking Him to send the crowd away so they could go into the villages and buy food for themselves. Jesus used the opportunity for a pop quiz. *"They don't need to go away," Jesus told them. "You give them something to eat"* (Matthew 14:16). John tells us that Jesus *asked this to test them, for he himself knew what he was going to do* (John 6:6). Philip estimated it would take 200 day's wages just to give everyone a little, and Andrew found a boy with five barley loaves and two fish. *"But what are they for so many?"* He asked. (John 6:7-9)

Philip focused on the cost, and Andrew only focused on their lack of resources. Neither had the faith that Jesus could make a difference. It was a humanly impossible task to accomplish. Their lack of faith caused them to see what they did not have, instead of looking to Jesus for the answer. They walked by sight rather than by faith.

The little boy with the bread and fish willingly gave all that he had to Jesus, not expecting anything in return. The disciples watched in eagerness, wondering what Jesus would do. Jesus blessed the food, broke it, and gave the pieces to the disciples to distribute to the people. Despite their lack of faith, the food multiplied. Everyone ate their fill, and twelve baskets of food were leftover.

You would think after seeing this miracle that all the people believed in Jesus. But they didn't. *Jesus realized that they were about to come and take him by force to make him king, he withdrew again to the mountain by himself* (John

6:15). The people wanted to make Jesus their king. And why not? He provided Free Education, Free Health Care, and Free Food. It was the ultimate welfare state!

Other than the resurrection, this is the only miracle Jesus performed recorded in all four Gospel accounts. It shows the importance of this day, as it marked a change in Jesus' ministry from focusing on the multitudes to mainly teaching and instructing His disciples. That night, Jesus and the disciples crossed the Sea of Galilee to the other side. During the night, Jesus once again revealed to the disciples He is the Son of God. In a powerful display of divine authority, Jesus walked on the water to meet the disciples in the boat.

The next morning when the people realized Jesus and the disciples were gone, they all followed to be with them again. John is the only gospel to record the events of this day, but the stark contrast from the previous day is important to note.

This time, Jesus was not so compassionate. Throughout His ministry, Jesus was critical and unsympathetic with the Pharisees, Sadducees, and other religious leaders who distorted the Word of God and placed undue burdens on the people. But with the general population, He was always understanding and compassionate—except for now.

On this day, Jesus said to them:
"Truly I tell you, you are looking for me, not because you saw the signs, but because you ate the loaves and were filled. Don't work for the food that perishes but for the food that lasts for eternal life, which the Son of Man will give you. ... I am the bread of life. No one who comes to me will ever be hungry, and no one who believes in me will ever be thirsty again. But as I told you, you've seen me, and yet you do not believe. ... Truly I tell you, anyone who believes has eternal life. I am the bread of life." (John 6: 26-27, 35-36, 47-48)

Jesus was more than a dispenser of food and medicine. He was their Savior. They wanted their physical needs met, but Jesus saw their spiritual emptiness. Their only concern was to have food on their tables, their sick healed, and to be entertained by the interesting stories Jesus told.

Certainly, we should be ready to care for the needs of the poor, just as Jesus fed the multitude and healed the sick. But that should not be our goal. Our purpose in caring for the poor and needy is so that we can bring them to a saving knowledge of Jesus Christ. Jesus is the only bread that can truly fill spiritual hunger.

After all this took place, it may surprise you to learn when many of His disciples heard this, they said, *"This teaching is hard. Who can accept it?" ... From that moment many of his disciples turned back and no longer accompanied him.* (John 6:60, 66)

Jesus had over twelve disciples. There were many followers being discipled by Jesus. At this point in His ministry, many of His disciples left. They said His teaching was too hard, they could not follow it. They came for the handouts and to be told feel-good stories. Not for spiritual renewal.

The Bible did not contain chapter and verse numbers until centuries after they were originally written. But I find it interesting that Revelation 13:18 tells us 666 is the number of man, and John 6:66 is about many disciples putting their own interest ahead of God's and stopped following Jesus.

Jesus said to the Twelve, "You don't want to go away too, do you?" Simon Peter answered, "Lord, to whom will we go? You have the words of eternal life. We have come to believe and know that you are the Holy One of God" (John 6:67-68).

It was after all the events of the past twenty-four hours, the twelve fully put their faith in Jesus as their Savior and Lord.

Before we become too critical of the crowds and the disciples who left, we need to examine our own life. Do we spend more time in prayer asking for physical needs or spiritual? Do we go to church to be entertained by the music and eloquent preaching? Paul warned Timothy, *For the time will come when people will not tolerate sound doctrine, but according to their own desires, will multiply teachers for themselves because they have an itch to hear what they want to hear* (2 Timothy 4:3).

Are you like the multitudes and disciples who turned away? Looking for a handout and a warm fuzzy feeling from a pastor preaching feel-good sermons. Or are you like the twelve in need of a Savior?

Prayer:

Dear Father in Heaven, we come before You today and ask Your forgiveness for the times that we lacked the faith to believe You could accomplish miracles in our lives. For the times we focused on what we did not have and not on what You can accomplish. May we not be like the multitudes who looked only at themselves, wanting all their physical needs met by You. Help us see our spiritual emptiness and the spiritual void in those around us and come to You for spiritual nourishment. Through Your Holy Spirit, provide us the strength and courage to lead others to You, the only Bread that truly satisfies. In the precious name of our Lord and Savior, we ask these things. Amen.

Action Steps

How have you encountered the Master Carpenter through today's narrative?

_____

_____

_____

_____

_____

What can you do to help others know this about Jesus?

_____

_____

_____

_____

_____

What might God be leading you to do based on this story in Scripture?

_____

_____

_____

_____

_____

Teach Us to Pray

Luke 11:1-13, Matthew 6:5-14

They grew up in the synagogue and had heard their local rabbi pray many times. They had heard the long self-edifying prayers of the Pharisees. No doubt their father had taught them the Shema as they said their morning prayers. Following Jewish custom, they prayed three times every day, morning prayers at sunrise, afternoon prayers at 3 pm (the time of the evening sacrifice in Jerusalem), and evening prayers at nightfall. They had studied the scriptures and knew the prayers of the prophets and could recite many of the prayers of King David from the Psalms. But no one had ever prayed like this man.

The teaching of Jesus amazed the disciples, for no one explained the scriptures as He did. They were in awe of the miracles He performed. But as they spent time with Him and listened to Him, as they watched what He did, they were impressed by His prayers. On one occasion when He had finished praying, His disciples asked, *"Lord, teach us to pray"* (Luke 11:1).

Nowhere is it recorded that the disciples ever ask Jesus to teach them to preach or minister more effectively. Scripture never mentions they ask how to study the Bible or tell parables imparting spiritual wisdom. But they asked Him to teach them to pray.

Our Lord was a Man of Prayer. He made prayer a priority, and the disciples saw Him praying often. Like many of us today, the disciples realized that the spiritual discipline they struggled with the most was prayer, and they wanted to learn from Jesus this secret of spiritual power and wisdom.

Jesus begins by giving them an example of prayer that we know as the Lord's Prayer. Here in Luke, the wording is a little different from the more familiar version that is recorded in Matthew, which was a year or two earlier in Jesus' ministry. However, the outline of the prayer is the same.

When we pray, we are to include:

➢ **Praise to God.**
Our Father in heaven, Hallowed be Your name (Luke 11:2a NKJV).

➢ **Pray for His ministry work to be done.**
Your kingdom come. Your will be done. On earth as it is in heaven (v. 2b NKJV).

➢ **We are to make request for ourselves and others.**
Give us day by day our daily bread (v. 3 NKJV).

➢ **We're to confess our sins.**
And forgive us our sins (v. 4a NKJV).

➢ **We are to seek His guidance and protection.**
And do not lead us into temptation, but deliver us from the evil one (v. 4b NKJV).

Jesus then tells them this parable of the persistent friend: *"Suppose one of you has a friend and goes to him at midnight and says to him, 'Friend, lend me three loaves of bread, because a friend of mine on a journey has come to me, and I don't have anything to offer him.' Then he will answer from inside and say, 'Don't bother me! The door is already locked, and my children and I have gone to bed. I can't get up to give you anything.' I tell you, even though he won't get up and give him anything because he is his friend, yet because of his friend's shameless boldness, he will get up and give him as much as he needs.* (Luke 11:5-8)

This parable is a wonderful reminder for our persistence in prayer. If an unrighteous man will give good gifts, how much more will our loving Father in heaven give us when we persistently asked.

When we pray, we are to ask and keep on asking, to seek and keep on seeking. We are to knock and keep on knocking (Luke 11:9-10). We are to keep in constant communication with our Father in Heaven. The Apostle Paul exhorted us to *pray constantly* (1 Thessalonians 5:17).

However, as important as the lesson on persistence in prayer is, we dare not miss the fundamental truth Jesus was teaching.

Did you notice who was with the man in the parable? Jesus said, *then he will answer from inside and say, "Don't bother me! The door is already locked, and my children and I have gone to bed. I can't get up to give you anything* (Luke 11:7).

The man was a father and was inside with his children. Do you think the man would have told one of his children to go away if they woke up during the night and asked for food or drink? Of course not!

Jesus concluded His teaching on prayer by saying, *What father among you, if his son asks for a fish, will give him a snake instead of a fish? Or if he asks for an egg, will give him a scorpion? If you then, who are evil, know how to give good gifts to your children, how much more will the heavenly Father give the Holy Spirit to those who ask him?* (Luke 11:11-13).

As Christians, we are God's children, and we don't have to worry about God turning us away. But how often do we act like the friend who had company drop in on him? We go through our day, seldom speaking to God. Then something unexpected happens in our lives, and in desperation we anxiously run to God, pounding on heaven's door. We feel helpless and alone and our prayers seem hollow. We knock harder and call out louder as if we must wake God up from His sleep. When the door finally opens, we pray, demanding a response from a seemingly reluctant God.

What a misrepresentation of who God is. We are not the desperate friend outside, franticly trying to get God's attention. We are inside, the dearly loved children. He is our loving Heavenly Father and desires to give us wonderful gifts if only we ask. We don't have to beat down heaven's doors. All we need to do is whisper. He is that close to us, and we are that dear to Him.

James, a half-brother of Jesus and early leader in the church at Jerusalem, was nicknamed 'Old Camel Knees' because his knees were extremely calloused from kneeling so often in prayer. He wrote: *You do not have because you do not ask. You ask and don't receive because you ask with wrong motives, so that you may spend it on your pleasures* (James 4:2b-3).

Prayer:

Dear Heavenly Father, we humbly come before Your throne in awe of who You are and of all You have done. Yet we are reminded You are our loving Father, and we are Your children. You desire for us to come to You seeking the good gifts You long to give us. Forgive us for all the times we struggle to pray. So often we feel as the disciples did that our prayer life is so inadequate. Teach us to come to You as a child with outstretched arms, running to their father for comfort. Help us through Your Holy Spirit to learn how to pray. In Christ's name, we pray. Amen.

Action Steps

Date _____

How have you encountered the Master Carpenter through today's narrative?

_____

_____

_____

_____

_____

What can you do to help others know this about Jesus?

_____

_____

_____

_____

_____

What might God be leading you to do based on this story in Scripture?

_____

_____

_____

_____

_____

Forgiven

John 8:2-11

It was early in the morning, and there was a peaceful stillness in the air. A moment in time, just waiting for the hustle and bustle of the day to erupt. As the sun crept above the horizon, it cast long shadows of the temple pillars across the courtyard. The only sound were the words of Jesus echoing through the temple as He taught those who gathered around Him.

We don't know what He taught that morning. It is not recorded in scripture. But the scene was abruptly and rudely interrupted as the religious leaders of the day laid a trap to catch Jesus. A sting operation, if you will, that was so carefully planned that they believed even Jesus could not escape. They had Him this time, and they knew they had Him. Or at least they thought they did.

As Jesus was teaching in the courtyard, the scribes and pharisees rudely and crudely interrupted Him. They brought a woman caught in the act of adultery, to be stoned according to the law of Moses. They snatched her out of her bed, forcibly pulling her away from her partner to bring her to Jesus.

Now that raises the question, where is the Man? If they caught her in the act of adultery, then he had to be there. He also would be guilty of adultery as well. But where is he now?

His absence leads us to see how this was a carefully planned trap. The woman did not matter to them. She was just a pawn to be used to fulfill their plan. They were not there for justice. They were there to trap Jesus and carefully planned every detail. Most likely, the man was there—one of the accusers!

The trap the religious leaders so carefully set, put Jesus in a seemingly no-win situation. If Jesus said to stone her, the people that were following Him would turn against Him. He taught to love one another, have compassion, and forgive each other. If He said to stone her, it would go against everything He taught throughout His ministry, and He would lose His followers.

However, if Jesus told the religious leaders to forgive her, then they had made their case. He would be guilty of breaking the law of Moses and they would have grounds for bringing their charges against Him.

The scribes and the Pharisees thought they had devised the perfect trap. But Jesus turned the tables on them. Without saying a word, He bent down and wrote with His finger on the ground. As He wrote, they continued to ask Him, taunting Him for an answer.

He stood up and said to them, *"The one without sin among you should be the first to throw a stone at her"* (John 8:7). As He spoke, His eyes connected with each of her accusers. A look from His eyes that penetrates all the way to the soul and sees the intent of the heart.

Once more, He bent down and wrote on the ground. We don't know what He wrote, but the Greek implies He wrote purposefully. Maybe He wrote accusations against those accusing the woman. He may have listed sins they had committed, possibly writing their name followed by a list of their sins.

The silence was deafening! Then, one by one, you could hear the thud of the stones hitting the ground. As one at a time, the men dropped their stones, turned, and walked away.

Jesus was left alone with the woman. Two people as different as different can be.

> The guilty and the guiltless.
> The accused and the judge.
> The one caught in sin and the one who was without sin.

She stood trembling before Jesus. Embarrassed by the situation she was found in, totally ashamed of her past life. Perhaps she was naked, or at most with a sheet clutched around her that she grasped as they dragged her away. She stood in utter humiliation.

Jesus asked, *"Woman, where are they? Has no one condemned you?" "No one, Lord,"* she answered. *"Neither do I condemn you,"* said Jesus. *"Go, and from now on do not sin anymore"* (John 8:10-11).

As you imagine that scene, place yourself in the woman's place. The Apostle John said, *if we say, "We have no sin," we are deceiving ourselves, and the truth is not in us. ... If we say, "We have not sinned," we make him a liar, and his word is not in us* (1 John 1:8, 10). Every one of us is like that woman. We have committed sins against God, and we need His forgiveness.

Like the woman, there will be a time when we will stand all alone, face to face with Jesus. Our pastor or Sunday School teacher will not be there to rely on for answers. Our spouse or parents can't defend us. It will be just you and Jesus.

It doesn't matter what the sin is. There is no sin so grievous that God's love is not great enough to offer forgiveness. John continued by saying, *if we confess our sins, he is faithful and righteous to forgive us our sins and to cleanse us from all unrighteousness* (1 John 1:9).

Scripture tells us that God will take our sin and separate it from us. *As far as the east is from the west, so far has he removed our transgressions from us.* (Psalm 103:12).

Jesus does not stand with a stone in His hand to condemn us. But His hands are no longer empty as they were that day. For they now contain the scars of His suffering for our sins. He is not only willing to forgive us, He is able.

As Christians, we not only need to seek God's forgiveness, but we also need to model His example and forgive others. *Just as the Lord has forgiven you, so you are also to forgive* (Colossians 3:13).

We first need to admit our own need for forgiveness. Then we need to extend it to others, asking God to help us forgive those who have wronged us. We are not to hold grudges or seek revenge. We are to trust God for justice and forgive the person who offended us.

Forgiving others is not for their benefit, it's for ours. For then we will be free from the thoughts of disappointment and bitterness and no longer live with the burden. Forgiving others releases us from resentment and allows God to give us the healing we need. An unforgiving, vengeful spirit stifles our daily walk with God and will separate us from the blessings that He intends for our life.

Forgiving others can be one of the hardest things we will ever do in this life. Certainly, the pain and hurt are real, and the thought of forgiveness may seem impossible. But the pain of living with the burden of bitterness and unforgiveness will quench the Spirit of God in our lives and ruin our relationship with others.

Prayer:

Dear Father, we come before Your throne as sinful people, and we are thankful for Your plan of salvation. We are forever grateful that Your Son was willing to come to earth and die for the forgiveness of our sins, and to set an example for us to forgive others. May Your Holy Spirit fill us, helping us from harboring hatred and bitterness in our hearts and truly forgive those who have hurt us. As we strive to follow His example, we pray these things in His name. Amen.

Action Steps

How have you encountered the Master Carpenter through today's narrative?

_____

_____

_____

_____

_____

What can you do to help others know this about Jesus?

_____

_____

_____

_____

_____

What might God be leading you to do based on this story in Scripture?

_____

_____

_____

_____

_____

Living in His Presence

John 15:1-11

As the sun setting beyond the western horizon brings an end to the day, this evening brought an end to Jesus' earthly ministry. For three and a half years, Jesus ministered traversing the countryside. Now on this night, He brings it all together in one grand crescendo of teaching. A time so insightful, so meaningful that sixty years later, as the Apostle John recounts the events of Jesus' ministry, he devotes one-fourth of his book on this single evening in the upper room.

The meal is finished, and Judas has left to prepare for the greatest act of treason the world will ever see. Jesus is now alone with the eleven remaining disciples. The flickering flames of torches on the wall illuminates the darkened room. The warm glow of light is matched by the warmth and love permeating from the Lord's face.

The cross is only a few hours away and soon He will ascend to the Father, leaving them on their own. Jesus uses this brief moment in time to encourage and instruct His select group of disciples. What words of wisdom would He impart to them? What is to be the secret to their success, the key to an effective ministry?

Jesus began His ministry with an invitation to come and follow Him. As His followers grew to tens of thousands, He further instructed them to be committed to and rely on Him. Now alone with His chosen few, He gives an additional command. If they are to be successful in ministry, if they are to take the gospel message to the world, they must abide in Him, and His Word must abide in them (John 15:4-6).

Therein lies the path to discipleship, the journey to maturity in Christ. The first recorded words of Jesus in the Gospel of John are, *"What are you looking for?"* In response to their answer, Jesus said, *"Come and you'll see"*. The next day, Jesus told them, *"Follow me"* (John 1:37 - 43). This is the place every one of us begins our journey with Christ. To everyone who is looking, Jesus invites them to come and see.

Then, as we take those first baby steps of faith, we follow Him. As our faith grows, we commit our lives and all that we are to Him and begin to rely on Him for our strength and well-being. As we continue to walk with Him, we learn to abide in Him, living in His presence.

Using the analogy of a vine and branches, Jesus vividly illustrates His point. *I am the vine; you are the branches. The one who remains in me and I in him produces much fruit, because you can do nothing without me* (John 15:5). Jesus is speaking intimately with His disciples, not the multitudes. The branches are those who have already established a relationship with Him, those who are connected to Him.

Abide In Him

A branch by itself is weak and useless. The branch must draw its life from the vine. Apart from the vine, the branch withers and dies. It is not enough to "plugin" to Christ for an hour or two on Sunday mornings. We must continually remain in Him for our spiritual life to grow and flourish.

Jesus desires a personal, intimate, close relationship with His followers, not just a superficial acquaintance. Through our prayers and meditating on His Word, we remain in constant communication with Him. Day by day, moment by moment, we are to walk with Him, focusing our thoughts and actions on Him.

It is our continual communion with Christ that empowers our spiritual life. Apart from Him, we can do nothing worthwhile for the Kingdom of God. When we abide in Him and allow Jesus to live His life through us, we can do anything He calls us to do.

His Word Abides in Us

Pastor R. A. Torrey declared, "If we are to obtain from God all that we ask from Him, Christ's words must abide or continue in us. We must study His words, fairly devour His words, let them sink into our thought and into our heart, keep them in our memory, obey them constantly in our life, let them shape and mold our daily life and our every act. This is really the method of abiding in Christ." [i]

The Psalmist wrote that he who delights *in the Lord's instruction, and he meditates on it day and night. He is like a tree planted beside flowing streams that bears its fruit in its season, and its leaf does not wither. Whatever he does prospers* (Psalm 1:2-3). A tree's roots bring constant nourishment and refreshment from the stream. Likewise, as we meditate day and night on God's Word, our spirits are refreshed, and we receive the nourishment needed for spiritual growth.

I will meditate on your precepts and think about your ways. I will delight in your statutes; I will not forget your word. ... How I love your instruction! It is my meditation all day long. Your command makes me wiser than my enemies, for it is always with me. I have more insight than all my teachers because your decrees are my

71

meditation. … Your word is a lamp for my feet and a light on my path. (Psalm 119:15-16, 97-99, 105)

It is not enough to read our Bibles and then forget what we've read as soon as we close the cover. The Words of God are to remain in our thoughts throughout the day as we allow the Holy Spirit to make them a part of our very life. As God's Word abides in us, His words become part of our vocabulary. His thoughts and precepts instinctively flow from within us.

Producing Abundant Fruit

Jesus did not command His disciples to produce fruit, but to abide. A branch by itself can't create a bud, much less real fruit. However, as it remains connected to the vine, sap flows naturally from the vine through the branches, producing abundant fruit. When we abide in Christ and His Word abides in us, His life flows through us and fruit develops.

The fruit Jesus is speaking of is the Christ-like qualities to be exhibited in the life of a disciple. Jesus told His disciples that evening, *Peace I leave with you. My peace I give to you* (John 14:27). He then tells them to *remain in my love … I have told you these things so that my joy may be in you and your joy may be complete* (John 15:9, 11).

The Apostle Paul informs us that love, joy, and peace are the first three fruits of the Spirit. *But the fruit of the Spirit is love, joy, peace, patience, kindness, goodness, faithfulness, gentleness, and self-control* (Galatians 3:22-23).

As we abide in Christ and His Word abides in us, these Christ-like characteristics are manifested in our lives. As they become established in our conduct, God is glorified, and Christ is made real to those around us. *My Father is glorified by this: that you produce much fruit and prove to be my disciples* (John 15:8).

Prayer:

Dear Father, forgive us for all the times we have tried to live our lives on our own, thinking we know what is best for our situations. Thank You for desiring to abide in us. Inspire in us the desire to live in Your presence, abiding in You and allowing Your Word to abide in us. May Your Spirit flow through us producing abundant fruit, bringing You glory as our lives develop the characteristics of Your Son, Jesus Christ. In His Name, we pray. Amen.

[i] R. A. Torrey, How to Pray (Chicago, IL: Moody, 1900), p59.

Action Steps

How have you encountered the Master Carpenter through today's narrative?

_____

_____

_____

_____

_____

What can you do to help others know this about Jesus?

_____

_____

_____

_____

_____

What might God be leading you to do based on this story in Scripture?

_____

_____

_____

_____

_____

Developing a
Consistent Prayer Life

Matthew 26:36-56

Peter, James, and John were abruptly awakened from their sleep. It had been a long week of teaching and ministering to the people, as well as debating with the Pharisees and other religious leaders. That evening they had a large meal with the other apostles, and now late into the night, slumber filled their eyes.

Worse than being awakened was the stinging rebuke that woke them. Words that cut so deep, they never forgot. *So, couldn't you stay awake with me one hour?* (Matthew 26:40).

Following their supper in the upper room, Jesus and His apostles had made their way across the Kidron Valley. There at the base of the Mount of Olives, they entered the peaceful Garden of Gethsemane, a favorite getaway of theirs.

On this night, Jesus told eight of His apostles to sit and wait near the garden gate. Peter, James, and John accompanied Jesus into the garden where He told them to watch and pray as He went a little further to talk with His Father alone.

As they entered the garden, the moon shone brightly through the twisted branches of the olive trees, decorating the garden with intertwined silhouettes appearing like a carpet of lace. The torches illuminating the city provided a warm, soft glow to the leaves as they fluttered in the cool, evening breeze. From one side of the garden, you could hear the voice of our Savior praying. But the only sound from the other side was the rhythmic snoring of three fishermen. The stark contrast of the events that followed stand as a powerful reminder of the necessity of prayer.

When the remaining person from their supper, Judas Iscariot, finally arrived at the garden, it wasn't to join them in prayer. He was accompanied by the religious leaders and soldiers who came to arrest Jesus.

While Jesus willfully submitted to them in accordance with His Father's will, Peter, fearing the crowd, drew a sword. Having no training as a soldier, he swung the sword like a fisherman casting a net. Trying to cut off a man's head, Peter missed so badly he merely clipped his ear (Matthew 26:51-56, John 18:10-11).

Earlier that night at supper, Peter had disputed with the Lord (Matthew 26:31-35), and then in the garden he disobeyed the Lord's command to pray (Matthew 26:40-41). Now he ran ahead of God, not waiting for the Lord's instructions, trusting his sword rather than God.

Jesus remained calm and at peace as the events unfolded throughout that night and early morning. In the garden, the apostles deserted Him, running in fear from the guards. As the night grew long, Peter, fearing the mob, turned on Jesus, denying he even knew Him! (Matthew 26:69-74, John 18:15-27).

The correlation is obvious. A consistent prayer life is necessary to remain in God's will and remain free of fear and worry.

Before we condemn Peter and the other apostles too harshly, we need to consider our own prayers. How often do we sleep better than we pray? How often do our minds wander when they should be watching? Certainly, the Lord could say to us as He said to Peter, *stay awake and pray, so that you won't enter into temptation. The spirit is willing, but the flesh is weak* (Matthew 26:41).

Pastor Adrian Rogers said, "The greatest privilege we have is prayer. The greatest failure that most of us have is prayer." [i] Regardless of what our prayer life is like, we can all stand to improve.

Peter certainly learned his lesson. Later he would write to Christians encouraging them as they suffered persecution and faced an uncertain future. He wrote, *the end of all things is near; therefore, be alert and sober-minded for prayer* (1 Peter 4:7). How similar are Peter's words to those of Jesus. We need to stay awake, be alert in our prayers, and pray with a sound mind.

The commanders of Israel's armies approached the prophet Jeremiah and said, *pray to the Lord your God on our behalf, on behalf of this entire remnant that the Lord your God may tell us the way we should go and the thing we should do* (Jeremiah 42:2-3).

Just like in Jeremiah's day, today we can discern God's plan for *the way we should go and the thing we should do* only when we pray. The more time we spend talking with God in prayer and reading His Word, the easier it is to walk in His ways and remain faithful and obedient to His perfect will.

The more we pray and stay in God's will, the less we need to worry and fear the events taking place in our lives. God said, *For I know the plans I have for you ... plans for your well-being, not for disaster, to give you a future and a hope* (Jeremiah 29:11).

God's plan for our lives is for our well-being, not for disaster—what do we have to fear? As we continue in prayer, we stay within God's plan of hope for the future.

Late in his life, while under house arrest chained to Roman guards and uncertain what the future held for him, the Apostle Paul emphasized the key to living a life free of anxiety and worry.

> *Don't worry about anything, but in everything, through prayer and petition with thanksgiving, present your requests to God. And the peace of God, which surpasses all understanding, will guard your hearts and minds in Christ Jesus.* (Philippians 4:6-7)

Paul says we are not to worry about anything. That is only possible if we pray about everything.

Pastor G. Campbell Morgan was once asked by a lady if she should bother God with prayers about all the little things in her life. He responded, "Madam, can you mention anything in your life that is big to God?" [ii]

Everything means everything. There is nothing in our lives that is too small for God's love to be concerned about, and there is nothing too big for God's power to handle.

When we continually pray to God about everything in our lives, we understand more fully God's will for our lives. When we stay within God's will for our lives, we can experience the peace of God as it guards our hearts and minds.

Even though our world may seem like it is crashing down around us, and others are running in fear, through our prayers we can rise above our circumstances and experience a peace and calmness that surpasses human comprehension and understanding.

Prayer:

Dear Heavenly Father, forgive us for all the times that our minds have wandered, and we have become distracted as we attempt to pray to You. We desire to spend time with You, but as Jesus told His apostles, so often our spirit is willing, but our flesh is weak.

We stand amazed at Christians we know and ones we have read about throughout history that are true prayer warriors and we desire to be like them. May Your Holy Spirit guide us as we develop a more fervent, effectual prayer life. Help us follow the example Jesus provided for us as we strive to improve our time in prayer. In His name, we ask these things, Amen.

[i] Adrian Rogers, "Prayer and the Will of God" lightsource.com/ministry/love-worth-finding/articles/prayer-and-the-will-of-god-12760.html

[ii] Dr. G. Campbell Morgan, as written in Thru the Bible. J. V. McGee. Nashville: Nelson, 1997.

Action Steps

How have you encountered the Master Carpenter through today's narrative?

_____

_____

_____

_____

What can you do to help others know this about Jesus?

_____

_____

_____

_____

What might God be leading you to do based on this story in Scripture?

_____

_____

_____

_____

_____

An Enviable Walk
with the Lord

Luke 24:13-35

It was Friday night and as the sun slipped behind the western horizon, the Sabbath would begin. It was a time of reverence and praise to God, but not on this night. The Sabbath during the Passover was a highlight of the year, but this year it was different. They were discouraged and dejected, and their hearts were not in their worship as they went through the motions.

As Friday turned into Saturday, their discouragement only intensified. Their hopes and dreams had been nailed to the cross with Jesus. He was to be their Messiah, their deliverer from the Roman bondage, but now He was dead. His words were so powerful and meaningful. His teaching was so captivating, so compelling. But now He was gone and what were they to do?

As the sun rose and broke through the clouds early that Sunday morning, some women went to the tomb. They said the tomb was empty, and they had seen a vision of angels who said He was alive. But it all seemed like nonsense.

Peter and John also went to the tomb and said He wasn't there. Talk of Him saying He would rise from the dead started to spread, but if that were true, where is He? He's not alive. He is just missing! Their discouragement turned to confusion and bewilderment. By Sunday afternoon, two of the followers had enough and started their journey home.

The late afternoon sun began to cast long shadows across the road as Cleopas and his wife made the long walk home. As they plodded along, they discussed the events of the past week. Questioning how it all went wrong and trying to make sense of it all. He healed others and raised the dead. Why could He not save Himself? They both had their opinions, and their discussion seemed more like a debate.

Then, as if from nowhere, a stranger appeared walking along with them. Stranger still, this man knew nothing of the things that had taken place in Jerusalem and asked them what they were arguing about.

Astonished by the visitor's ignorance of current events, the couple stopped still. With sadness written across their face, they explained the terrible event that happened to Jesus, the prophet from Nazareth, who taught with understanding and had performed incredible miracles. They had put their hope in Him. He was to be the Messiah and would rescue Israel.

Brokenhearted, they explained how He was arrested, condemned to death, and was crucified. And if that wasn't enough, now His body is missing, and no one knows where He is.

The stranger rebuked them, saying, *"How foolish you are, and how slow to believe all that the prophets have spoken!"* (Luke 24:25).

As they traveled to Emmaus, the stranger walked with them and explained the scriptures to them. Without notes or opening a scroll, He quoted scripture beginning with

Genesis, the first book of Moses, He taught through the books of history and poetry as well as all the Prophets. He interpreted for them the things concerning the Messiah written in all the Scriptures.

The couple had never heard the Scriptures explained so clearly and with such understanding. The journey to Emmaus seemed to take no time at all. When they reached their home, they urged the stranger to stay with them, as it was late at night.

It was the custom of that day for the host to serve food to their guest. But the two disciples had little interest in food, they wanted to hear more teaching from this most unusual stranger. The only bread they were interested in was the bread of life. They hungered and thirsted for understanding from the Word of God.

The stranger, taking the place of a servant, served the meal. As they reclined at the table for supper, He took the bread, blessed and broke it, and gave it to them. As He reached out His hands—there it was.

Could it really be? No, of course not. He is dead! But there on His hands, the scars from the nails were plainly visible. Was this truly the risen Savior?

Their gaze lifted from His hands and as they looked into His loving eyes, their eyes were opened, and they recognized Him. As the couple was staring into the face of their Savior, instantly Jesus disappeared from their sight.

Cleopas turned to his wife and beaming with joy they said to each other in perfect unison as if their thoughts were aligned, *"Weren't our hearts burning within us while he was talking with us on the road and explaining the Scriptures to us?"* (Luke 24:32)

That very hour, without wasting a moment, they got up and returned to Jerusalem—they had to go tell someone.

It did not matter they had not eaten—they had to go tell someone.

It did not matter it was late at night and time for sleep—they had to go tell someone.

It did not matter Jerusalem was a two-hour climb up a mountain on a rocky and dangerous road—they had to go tell someone.

It did not matter there were thieves and robbers along the way—they had to go tell someone.

They had seen the risen Savior. Their Messiah was indeed alive! Their hearts were burning within them—they had to go tell someone.

How wonderful the teaching of Jesus on the road to Emmaus must have been. A complete Bible survey class taught by Jesus Himself. But we don't have to be envious of these two disciples. Jesus said, *I have spoken these things to you while I remain with you. But the Counselor, the Holy Spirit, whom the Father will send in my name, will teach you all things and remind you of everything I have told you* (John 14:25-26).

The very same Holy Spirit that inspired the Apostles and Prophets to write the Bible dwells within every Believer. Don't you think He knows it well enough to explain it to you?

The Psalmist said, *I will meditate on your precepts and think about your ways. ... Open my eyes so that I may contemplate wondrous things from your instruction* (Psalms 119:15, 18). As we read our Bible, we need to ask God to open our eyes to comprehend what He has written. Then, throughout our day, as we meditate and think about what we have read, the Holy Spirit will help us understand the meaning of the Scripture and, more importantly, its application to our lives.

We don't have to be envious of the disciples on the road to Emmaus. God desires to walk with us every day and give us an understanding of His Word and how to apply it to our lives. Learning Bible knowledge can lead to a big head, but receiving Biblical truth and walking with the Savior will lead to a burning heart!

The more we receive the Word of God, the more we will want to fellowship with the God of the Word. Scripture will come alive for us, and our hearts will burn within us. And like those Emmaus Disciples of long ago, we will have to go tell somebody!

Prayer:

Dear Father, we thank You for the truth You have given us in Your Word, and for sending us Your Holy Spirit to guide us in understanding and comprehending Your Holy Scriptures. Instill within us the desire to read and meditate on Your Word daily. Fill us with that same fire, that same exciting joy that filled the two disciples on the road to Emmaus, so that like them, we will have an all-encompassing desire to tell someone about You. In Christ's name, we pray. Amen.

Action Steps

How have you encountered the Master Carpenter through today's narrative?

_____

_____

_____

_____

_____

What can you do to help others know this about Jesus?

_____

_____

_____

_____

_____

What might God be leading you to do based on this story in Scripture?

_____

_____

_____

_____

_____

_____

Fully Restored

John 21:1-19

To the disciples and those who followed Jesus closely, the cross signaled defeat. They believed Jesus was their Messiah, the one who would deliver them from Roman bondage. But as Jesus hung on that cross and died, the Romans once again had their way. They were the victors. Instead of the peace and joy that Jesus so often spoke about, only doubt and discouragement filled their hearts.

Certainly, on Sunday morning finding His tomb empty, brought them some hope. And Jesus appeared to them that evening, bringing joy to their hearts, but then He disappeared. It was a full week before any of them saw Him again. This time Thomas was with them, and Jesus told him, *put your finger here and look at my hands. Reach out your hand and put it into my side. Don't be faithless, but believe* (John 20:27).

The disciples wanted to believe. They knew they should. While they could not understand or comprehend, they knew somehow, some way, Jesus arose from the dead. He was alive. But where is He now?

They traveled to Galilee as Jesus instructed them to do. Three and a half years earlier, Jesus started His ministry there. Maybe now in Galilee He will establish His Kingdom. But Jesus was nowhere to be found. Feeling all alone without their leader, their doubt and discouragement turned to despair and disappointment.

Finally, Peter had enough. *I'm going fishing* (John 21:3), he told the others. Six of the disciples joined him.

It was a quiet night as they sailed on the Sea of Galilee. The moon and stars shone brightly as they cast their nets out into the water. The scene was all too familiar to them. They were all professional fishermen and fished these waters regularly before Jesus called them to be His disciples. But the quiet night and familiarity of fishing could not quiet Peter's mind.

His mind raced with memories. Memories of Him. It was here on these waters that twice Jesus calmed the storm. And over there, Peter actually stepped out of the boat and walked on the water with Him. There on the shore is where Jesus fed the five thousand and healed so many with diseases. Peter remembered all the amazing stories He told, and the time Jesus had him catch a fish and take a coin from its mouth to pay their taxes.

As Peter pulled on the nets dragging them on board, then casting them back out into the water, he tried to forget. But the memories kept coming back. So many memories. So many wonderful times he spent with Jesus. But for what?

As the hours passed and he dragged in empty net after empty net, another memory filled his mind he wished he could forget. That of fishing all night and not catching any fish!

As the night faded away and the sun sneaked above the horizon, they could make out a man on shore. He was calling to them, asking if they had caught any fish. "No," the disciples replied. *"Cast the net on the right side of the boat,"* he told them, *"and you'll find some"* (John 21:6). The disciples did, and their nets were so full of fish they could barely pull it in.

As Peter was busy pulling on the ropes with all his might to haul in the nets, John exclaims, *"It is the Lord"* (John 21:7). Without a moment's hesitation, Peter leaves the nets behind and dives into the water, swimming to the shore.

Wet and shivering from the cold water, Peter stands by the fire Jesus had made. As the water from his wet hair ran down his face and dripped off his beard, Peter had another memory of standing by another fire just a few weeks earlier. Peter had promised Jesus, he would never leave Him. Even if he had to die, Peter said he would not disown Jesus. Yet just a few hours later, standing by that fire in the courtyard in Jerusalem, Peter denied Jesus three times, cursing and swearing he did not know Him.

While the others struggled to bring the boat and nets of fish ashore, Peter stood there alone with Jesus, just the two of them. The very presence of his friend and mentor certainly filled him with joy, yet doubt and uncertainty surely occupied his mind. What would Jesus say to him? Would He call him a failure? Would He reprimand Peter for what he had done? Would He say how disappointed He was in Peter's behavior?

Jesus remained silent and allowed His friend to warm and dry himself by the fire. As the others arrive on shore, Jesus invites them all to have breakfast.

Once Peter's physical needs are met, Jesus takes him aside. He simply asks Peter if he loves Him. Jesus asks Peter the same question three times, once for each of Peter's denials.

Each time Peter responds in the affirmative, and each time Jesus tells Peter to shepherd and feed His flock. With that, Peter knows all is forgiven. All is right with his Lord. In the most loving and inspiring way, Peter's faith is restored, and his Lord has called him to a ministry in leading and discipling His followers.

Regardless of how badly we have sinned, how badly we have behaved, just like Peter, Jesus is standing beside us, willing to forgive us. *If we confess our sins, he is faithful and righteous to forgive us our sins and to cleanse us from all unrighteousness* (1 John 1:9).

It does not matter if we have memories of better times in the past when we were effective in ministry and feel all alone and useless. Just like Peter, Jesus still has a purpose for our lives and has a ministry for us to fulfill.

As the Apostle Paul told Timothy, *He has saved us and called us with a holy calling, not according to our works, but according to his own purpose and grace, which was given to us in Christ Jesus before time began. ... As for you, exercise self-control in everything, endure hardship, do the work of an evangelist, fulfill your ministry* (2 Timothy 1:9, 4:5).

What greater testimony can be made of our lives than to say along with Paul, *I have fought the good fight, I have finished the race, I have kept the faith. There is reserved for me the crown of righteousness, which the Lord, the righteous Judge, will give me on that day, and not only to me, but to all those who have loved his appearing* (2 Timothy 4:7-8).

Prayer:
Dear Father, as we come before You today, we admit often we feel like Peter must have felt that day. We know in the past we have disappointed You with our words and behavior, and we ask Your forgiveness. We have memories of better times, times of effective ministry for You. But now we feel alone and discouraged. Help us take our eyes off the past and look forward to the future. Inspire us with Your plans for service and ministry, and may we always walk with You, keeping our eyes on our Lord and Savior Jesus Christ. In His name, we pray. Amen.

Action Steps

How have you encountered the Master Carpenter through today's narrative?

_____

_____

_____

_____

_____

What can you do to help others know this about Jesus?

_____

_____

_____

_____

_____

What might God be leading you to do based on this story in Scripture?

_____

_____

_____

_____

_____

Follow Me

John 21:20-23

The twentieth chapter of John seems to be the crowning ending to Jesus' story. He arose from the grave victoriously, Jesus appeared to His disciples, and He commissioned them. John then gives his purpose for writing his Gospel.

> *Jesus performed many other signs in the presence of his disciples that are not written in this book. But these are written so that you may believe that Jesus is the Messiah, the Son of God, and that by believing you may have life in his name* (John 20:30-31).

It appears to be anti-climactic to write anything more. But John wrote sixty years after these events took place and there was one more story to be told. How did his close friend and companion Peter go from the confused, disillusioned disciple who denied even knowing Jesus, to become the confident, courageous church leader we read about in the book of Acts?

Two weeks passed since the crucifixion. Jesus appeared to the disciples occasionally but left as quickly as He arrived. Discouraged and uncertain of their future, Peter persuaded six other disciples to go fishing with him. This was not a weekend of rest and relaxation on the lake. They set out to return to their previous occupation as fishermen.

After an unsuccessful night of fishing, Jesus greeted them from the shore and served them breakfast. Jesus then called Peter aside, and in the most beautiful way, restored the faith of Peter.

Peter had denied Jesus three times and three times Jesus asks Peter if he loved Him. Each time Jesus gave instruction for Peter's ministry, Feed My Lambs, Shepherd My Sheep, Feed My Sheep. Then Jesus must have shock Peter as He told him how he would die. No doubt, Peter rejoiced that he was restored to fellowship, but why bring up martyrdom?

Peter had one more lesson to learn. Jesus had taken Peter aside and spoke to him privately, instead of in front of the other disciples. But John got curious. He followed behind them, listening.

Hearing John getting closer, Peter turned to see him. Peter took his eyes off Jesus and looked at John and asked, *"Lord, what about him?"* (John 21:21).

Jesus had just told Peter to follow Him, but a fellow believer distracted him. Instead of looking to Jesus and following God's plan for his life and ministry, he became preoccupied by what God was doing with someone else.

Sometimes, we do that. We are told something that is uncomfortable to hear, and we point to someone else. We compare ourselves with others. God wants us to follow Him, not other believers. We are to identify ourselves with Jesus, not other Christians.

One of the fastest ways to discourage yourself and fall into sin is by comparing yourself to others. It is a hard lesson to learn. It's just human nature to compare our behavior with others, but we can take it too far. We can see the disastrous results of people who compared themselves to others throughout the Bible.

Cain compared his offering to Abel's and ended up killing his brother (Genesis 4:1-16). Jacob and Esau compared themselves to each other and tore their family apart (Genesis 25-27). The nation Israel compared themselves to other nations and demanded a king, resulting in turning away from God and eventually being led into exile (1 Samuel 8). To name just a few.

If you try to follow Jesus while looking over your shoulder to see what direction other Christians are going, eventually, you are going to stumble. The Apostle Paul said, *let each person examine his own work, and then he can take pride in himself alone, and not compare himself with someone else. For each person will have to carry his own load* (Galatians 6:4-5).

God has a plan for your life, and you will never accomplish His plan by looking at others. God doesn't deal with us comparatively, but with each of us individually.

Peter made the mistake of taking his eyes off the Lord twice before. After the great catch of fish when Jesus first came to him, Peter realized who he was and took his eyes off Jesus. He looked at himself saying, *"Go away from me, because I'm a sinful man, Lord!"* (Luke 5:8). He took his eyes off Jesus and looked at himself.

We may look at ourselves and make excuses of why we cannot do something. Moses had that problem. When God called him to go to Egypt and free His people, Moses made excuses for a chapter and a half (Exodus 3-4). Some of us are so good at giving excuses, we make Moses look like an amateur. When we look at our shortfalls and inabilities and take our eyes off Jesus, it is easy to say, "I can't do that, that's not for me".

The Apostle Paul said, *I am able to do all things through him who strengthens me* (Philippians 4:13). It's not our abilities that allow us to minister for God. It is Christ working through the Holy Spirit in us which allow us to accomplish anything for God. We must take our eyes off ourselves and keep focused on Jesus.

Then when Peter walked on the water, he took his eyes off Jesus again. The wind and waves distracted him and immediately he sank. It is dangerous to focus on our circumstances instead of looking to God.

The great prophet Elijah started his ministry with courage and valor. Fearlessly, he stood against King Ahab and the prophets of Baal on Mt. Carmel. But then he took his eyes off the Lord. Focusing on the surrounding threats from Jezebel, he ran for his life and hid in a cave (1 Kings 18:20-19:18).

It's easy to see the circumstances around us and focus on what we can't do instead of keeping our eyes on Jesus. The Apostle Paul said, *Set your minds on things above, not on earthly things* (Colossians 3:2).

To be distracted by ourselves, our circumstances, or by other Christians is to disobey the Lord. Jesus rebuked Peter and reminded him it was not his job to interfere in the lives of other Believers. *"If I want him to remain until I come," Jesus answered, "what is that to you? As for you, you follow me"* (John 21:22).

Peter was to follow Jesus and Him alone. As we discover in the book of Acts, Peter followed the Lord's leading and as a result fulfilled a powerful, effective ministry. He learned his lesson and serves as an outstanding example for us to follow.

We need to keep our eyes of faith on Jesus and on Him alone. God has a ministry for each of us to perform. If we keep our eyes on the Lord and not on ourselves, our circumstances, or others, God may accomplish miraculous things through us.

Prayer:

Dear Father, as we come before You today, help us keep from taking our eyes off You and looking at what other Christians are doing. Help us keep from being distracted by our short comings and failures or distracted by what is happening in our lives and the circumstances around us. Inspire us with Your plans for service and ministry You have for us. And may we always walk with You, keeping our eyes focused on our Lord and Savior Jesus Christ. In His name, we pray, Amen.

Action Steps

Date _____

How have you encountered the Master Carpenter through today's narrative?

_____

_____

_____

_____

What can you do to help others know this about Jesus?

_____

_____

_____

_____

What might God be leading you to do based on this story in Scripture?

_____

_____

_____

_____

_____

Scripture Index

About the Author

With a unique blend of storytelling and Bible exposition, Brad Simon has shared God's Word for over forty-five years. He is founder and director of Christian Growth Ministry, working to encourage believers to mature in their walk with Christ, grow in their faith, and serve in ministry, all for the glory of God.

Brad Simon is the featured Bible Teacher on Monday Morning Inspiration, a podcast designed to inspire listeners to experience life with God more deeply. He is also a frequent contributor to Refresh Bible Study Magazine and has written devotional articles for book compilations and blogs.

Brad is a retired Master Jeweler. He relies on the God-given creativity that won him several national and international jewelry design awards to craft Biblical Narratives and Life Stories that are engaging and thought-provoking. Once a speaker, author, publisher, and trainer for the jewelry industry, now he is putting those skills to work to promote the beauty and appeal of God's Word.

Originally from Illinois, Brad and his wife Debbie have made Spartanburg, South Carolina, their home for the past twenty-five years. They are proud parents of two sons (one married) and two grandsons. His one guilty pleasure is being an avid fan of St. Louis Cardinals baseball.

Discover his Bible Teaching Ministry at:
BWSimon.com
Facebook.com/BradSimonTeachingMinistry

Do you struggle with your prayers?

So did the Apostles!

Jesus taught His disciples to pray, yet they continued to struggle. Then as we turn to the Book of Acts, we find the prayers of the Apostles at the heart of transforming their ministry, as these common ordinary fishermen became the spiritual giants who turned the world upside down.

Discover the life-changing Power of Prayer
in the lives of the Apostles.

Encounters with God through Prayer
written by *Brad Simon*

!

Go To: ChristianGrowthMinistry.com/prayer

Discover additional books by author Brad Simon at:
BWSimon.com/books

Monday Morning Inspiration

Join Bible Teacher Brad Simon as Christian Growth Ministry presents Monday Morning Inspiration a Podcast designed to inspire you to grow in the faith and encourage you to walk closer with the Lord. Listen during your drive time or anytime for Inspiration from God's Word.

Listen at: ChristianGrowthMinistry.com
or on your favorite Podcast App.

Working to Encourage Believers to Mature in Their Walk with Christ, Grow in Their Faith, & Serve in Ministry, All for the Glory of God.

ChristianGrowthMinistry.com

Facebook.com/ChristianGrowthMinistries

Refresh Bible Study Magazine

Connecting God's Word to Life Today

*Discover stories, Scripture,
and strategies for the Christian life.*

The mission of Refresh is to connect God's Word to life today. This free, digital magazine published by Lighthouse Bible Studies is sent quarterly to subscribers. Use Refresh for personal encouragement or for small group discussion. Use some of the stories, quotes, or topics as conversation starters to get people talking about God and His Word.

Brad Simon is a frequent contributor to Refresh Magazine. You can receive a free subscription at: LighthouseBibleStudies.com/refresh-bible-study-magazine

Come join us for "Be Refreshed," a weekly discussion of Refresh articles. We meet on Zoom on Thursdays from 7-8 pm eastern time, and hear an author read his or her article, and we discuss it.

To receive the link for the zoom online group E-mail: LighthouseBibleStudies@hotmail.com

Made in the USA
Columbia, SC
12 February 2024

31327435R00072